n e w   s e a s o n s ®

New Seasons is a registered trademark of Publications International, Ltd.

Written by Nicole Sulgit

Photography from: Shutterstock.com

Louis Weber, CEO
Publications International, Ltd.
8140 Lehigh Avenue
Morton Grove, IL 60053

www.pilbooks.com

Manufactured in Canada.

8 7 6 5 4 3 2 1

ISBN: 978-1-64030-713-1

Mother
L🐾VE

There's no better way to enjoy
a beautiful day than to spend it
with you!

Mom? Do you want to play?

How about now?

The furry cuteness comes from my side of the family.

I'm totally winning this game, Mom!

Countless spots, endless love.

Family gives you strength.

No matter how old you are or where you go, you'll always *bee* my favorite.

Seeing you happy
brings me joy.

Even when the world is big and noisy,
I know I'm safe with you, Mom.

You try getting six puppies to look at
a camera at the same time.

I love you more than anything.

Love isn't halved with two children.

It's doubled.

Mom, you're always there when I'm feeling down. Thanks.

You're my sunshine on rainy days.

Mama, I'm going to take a nap
with you!

You're both my favorite children, now stop howling about it!

Warm cuddles, cheerful dreams.

It doesn't matter how big you grow.
You'll always be my baby.

Let's play a game to see who can sit
still for the longest.

You say you aren't tired, but I think it might be time for bed.

Each of you is precious in my heart.

We're ready for our closeup.

You say you found a shoe to chew?

I call this family
meeting to attention.

It's not a secret that I love you.

Shared days, shared stories,
shared memories.

What could be better than a nap in the sunshine with the ones you love?

When we're not sure where to go,

Mom shows us the way.

Look out at the camera, darlings. No,
the camera isn't under my chin.

Good naps make for blue-ribbon days.

I'm going to look just like Mom when I grow up!

Any time is a good time for cuddle time!

Mom, whatever my goal, I know you've got my back. Thank you.

We're lucky that warm fur is a family trait.

My biggest treasure came in a very small package.

Don't worry. I'm here for you.

All right, here's our plan for getting treats from our human.

Lazy days are happy days.

Mom, I know I'm lucky that I can tell you anything.

You don't think the humans will mind that
I ate their hamburgers, do you? Mom?

Family stands together.

Oooh, Mom, neat stick! Can I share?

I can absolutely see where
we're going.

Of course we're behaving! Why would you think we're not behaving?

Mom, I think you need a nap, too.

Mom, you showed me how to see wonders
in the world around me.

Here's the plan. On three, we wag our tails and give the humans our best puppy dog look.

Mom, thanks for standing guard so I could grow and play and dream.

Just being around you brings me joy.

I always want to take
you with me.

I know you said it was naptime, but I think
it might be playtime?

Love you!